FOURTH
BOOK OF IMPORTANT
DATES

ILLUSTRATED WITH
ELEANOR GILPATRICK'S
PAINTINGS OF
ABSTRACTS, STILL LIFES, AND
NEBULAS

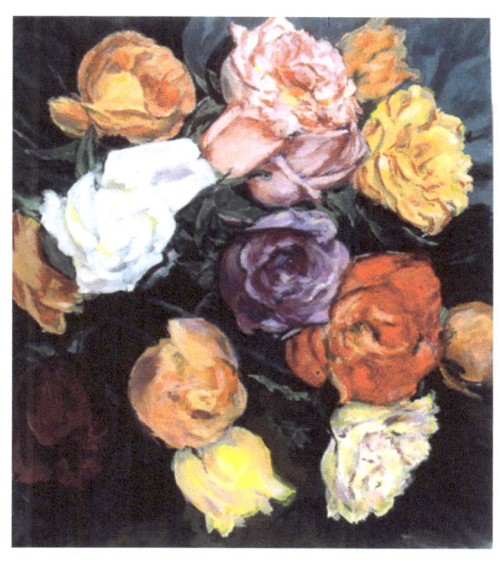

PLEASE NOTE:

The images presented in this book are based on the RGB color system, used when digital images are produced from photographs of paintings. With publication in a book, the CMYK color system is used. Documents that move from a computer screen to a printed page are affected by the fact that there are RGB colors that CMYK printers cannot reproduce. Something that looks good on a monitor may not look the same when printed. To overcome this limitation I have reviewed each printed page in a proof copy, and have made changes to bring the printed pages into as close a representation of the actual paintings as possible.

But the process is not perfect; and a small amount of variance from unit to unit is expected. The color may vary slightly from print run to print run and day to day.

I hope that you will enjoy this book; I encourage you to view the online website where images of the paintings are presented: http://www.Zibbet.com/Egilpatr

Eleanor Gilpatrick

Cover Image:
Spray; 28 x 38 inches

Title Page Image:
He Brought Me Roses; 20 x 17 inches

Biography Page Image:
Melnik Echoes; 13 x 29 inches

Book design: Eleanor Gilpatrick

ISBN: 1448675707
EAN-13: 9781448675708

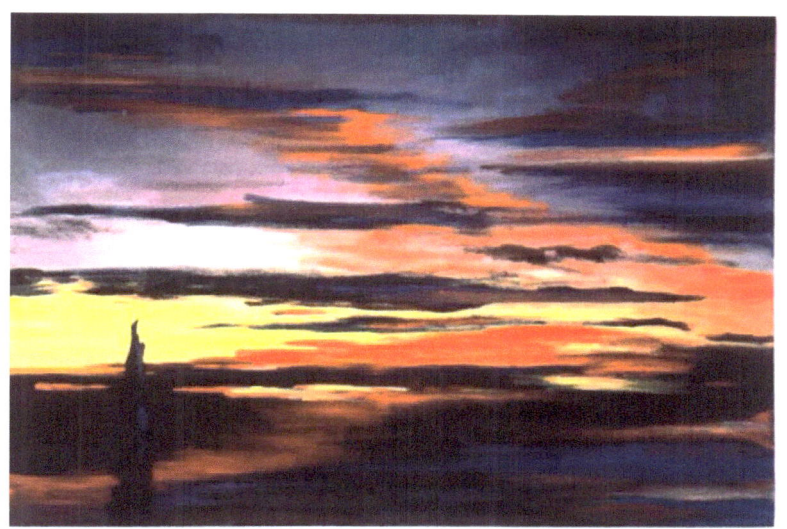

JANUARY

For me, abstracts and nebulas are about space and flow. Of course, they are different in scale, but they allow me broad brushstrokes and free movement. They are a kind of counterpoint to my more representational works.

From Sandia was inspired by a visit to the Sandia Mountains near Albuquerque, NM. We took a cable car ride to a restaurant at the top at sunset, and this was my abstract response to the vista. The painting is 32 inches high by 46 inches wide, acrylic on stretched canvas, on heavy duty stretchers, with painted sides. It is on view at http://www.Zibbet.com/Egilpatr

JANUARY

1_____

2_____

3_____

4_____

5_____

6_____

7_____

8_____

9_____

10_____

11_____

12_____

13_____

14_____

15_____

16_____

JANUARY

17 _____

18 _____

19 _____

20 _____

21 _____

22 _____

23 _____

24 _____

25 _____

26 _____

27 _____

28 _____

29 _____

30 _____

31 _____

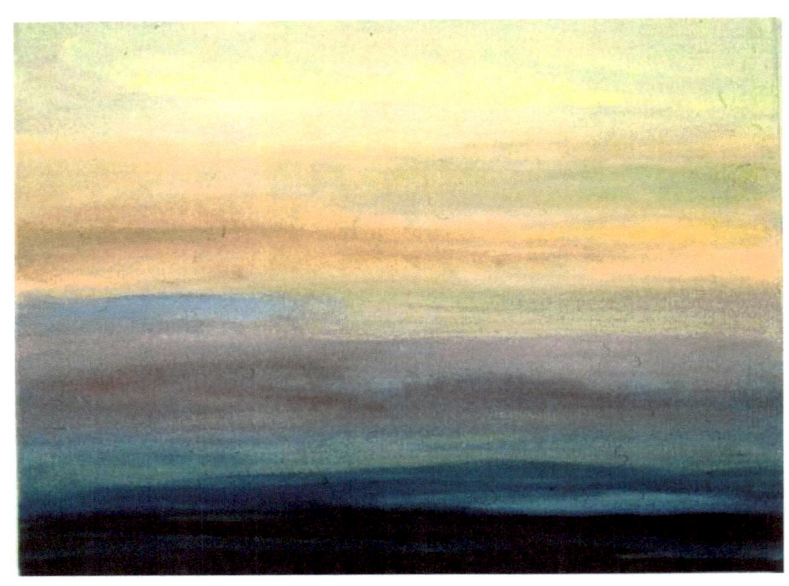

FEBRUARY

Sky Lights was created while I was working on another painting set in Montauk, NY. I was attracted to the gentle colors of the sunset sky; and this painting expresses the look of the light. The painting is 12 inches high by 16 inches wide, acrylic on stretched canvas, on heavy duty stretchers, with painted sides. It can be seen at http://www.Zibbet.com/Egilpatr

FEBRUARY

1 _____

2 _____

3 _____

4 _____

5 _____

6 _____

7 _____

8 _____

9 _____

10 _____

11 _____

12 _____

13 _____

14 _____

15 _____

16 _____

FEBRUARY

17 _____

18 _____

19 _____

20 _____

21 _____

22 _____

23 _____

24 _____

25 _____

26 _____

27 _____

28 _____

29 LEAP YEAR! _____

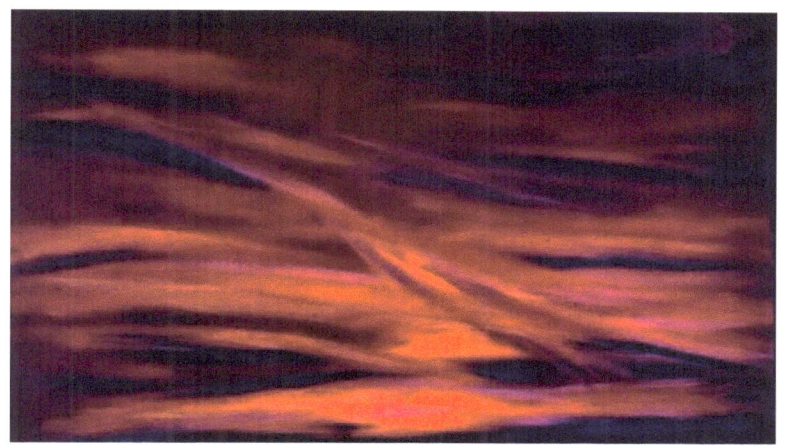

MARCH

Seeing Red, Homage to Gabriele, is an homage to Gabriele Evertz, with whom I studied at Hunter College, New York City. She curated an art show about the use of red in modern art. This is a red abstract/sunset/landscape inspired by her show. The painting is 28 inches high by 46 inches wide, acrylic on stretched canvas on heavy duty stretchers, with painted sides. It can be seen at http://www.Zibbet.com/Egilpatr

MARCH

1 _____

2 _____

3 _____

4 _____

5 _____

6 _____

7 _____

8 _____

9 _____

10 _____

11 _____

12 _____

13 _____

14 _____

15 _____

16 _____

MARCH

17 _____

18 _____

19 _____

20 _____

21 _____

22 _____

23 _____

24 _____

25 _____

26 _____

27 _____

28 _____

29 _____

30 _____

31 _____

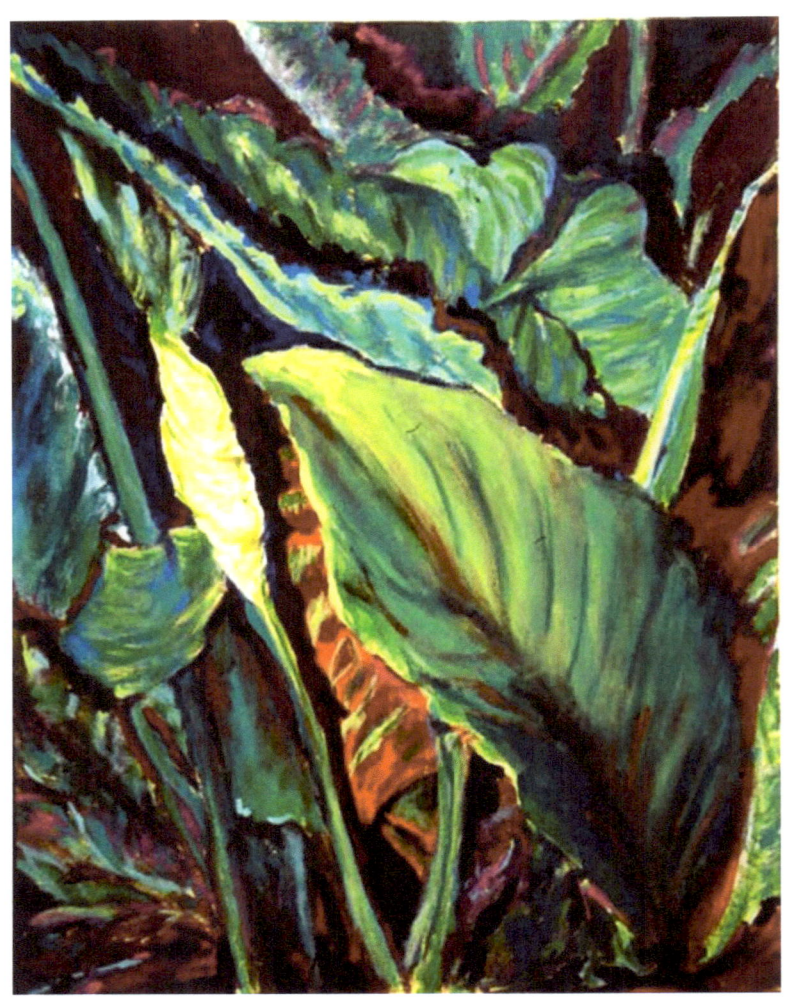

APRIL

Please Don't Leaf Me is a still life that helps me remember a leafy plant that was sent to me when I had suffered a loss. The title is a wry pun. The painting is 26 inches high by 20 inches wide, acrylic on stretched canvas. The framed dimensions are 28 by 22 inches. See it at http://www.Zibbet.com/Egilpatr

APRIL

1 _____

2 _____

3 _____

4 _____

5 _____

6 _____

7 _____

8 _____

9 _____

10 _____

11 _____

12 _____

13 _____

14 _____

15 _____

16 _____

APRIL

17 _____

18 _____

19 _____

20 _____

21 _____

22 _____

23 _____

24 _____

25 _____

26 _____

27 _____

28 _____

29 _____

30 _____

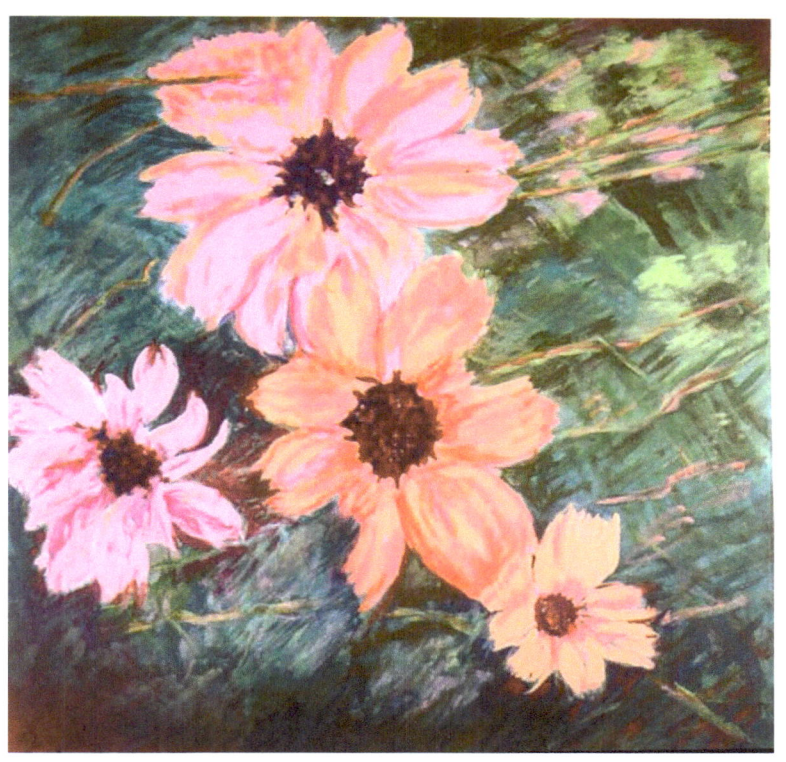

MAY

Look is an abstract, floral still-life painting with a deliberately limited palette. Here are flowers from another point of view. The painting is 36 by 36 inches, acrylic on stretched canvas, and it is framed. The framed dimensions are 38 by 38 inches. The original painting can be seen online at http://www.Zibbet.com/Egilpatr

MAY

1 _____

2 _____

3 _____

4 _____

5 _____

6 _____

7 _____

8 _____

9 _____

10 _____

11 _____

12 _____

13 _____

14 _____

15 _____

16 _____

MAY

17 _____

18 _____

19 _____

20 _____

21 _____

22 _____

23 _____

24 _____

25 _____

26 _____

27 _____

28 _____

29 _____

30 _____

31 _____

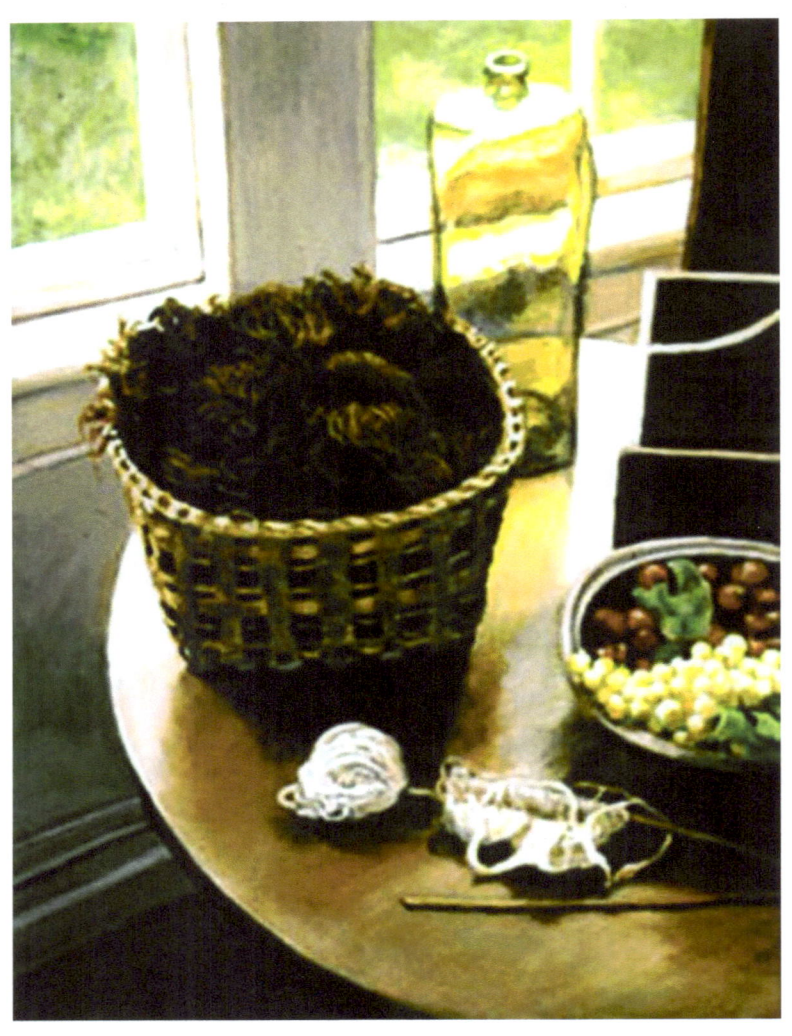

JUNE

Still Life With Yarn, Circa 1750, is based on a display in The Mulford House in East Hampton, New York, which is restored and open to the public. I was captured by the old yarn and the glass. The painting is 20 inches high by 15 inches wide, acrylic on stretched canvas on heavy duty stretchers, with painted sides. The painting can be seen online at this website: http://www.Zibbet.com/Egilpatr

JUNE

1 _____

2 _____

3 _____

4 _____

5 _____

6 _____

7 _____

8 _____

9 _____

10 _____

11 _____

12 _____

13 _____

14 _____

15 _____

16 _____

JUNE

17 _____

18 _____

19 _____

20 _____

21 _____

22 _____

23 _____

24 _____

25 _____

26 _____

27 _____

28 _____

29 _____

30 _____

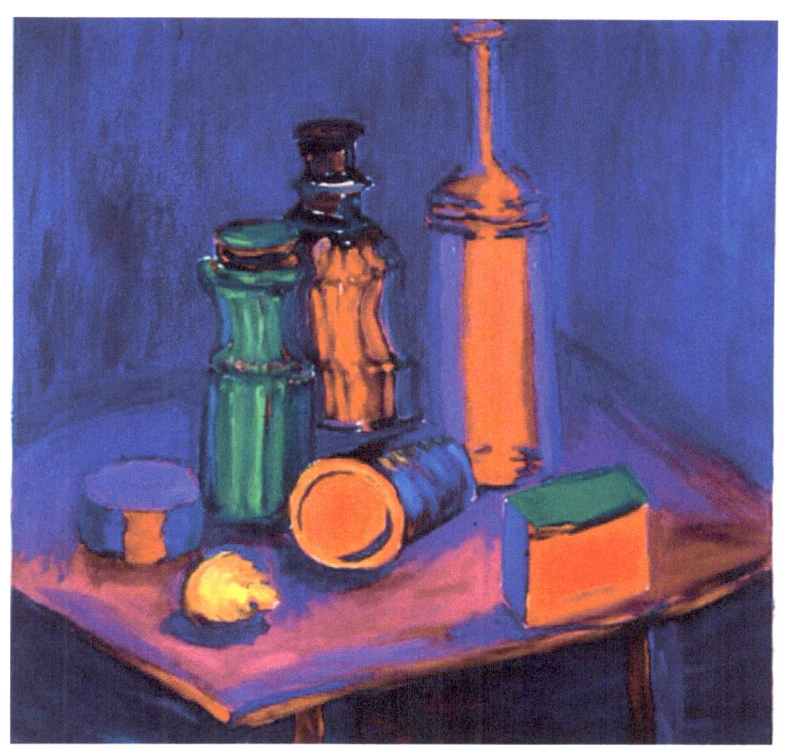

JULY

The title, **Hue Go Your Way**, is a pun. This still life depends on hue and color theory to create shape, depth, and focus and is a bit fauvist in rendering.

It is 48 by 48 inches, oil on stretched canvas, on heavy duty stretchers, with painted sides. You can see it online at this website: http://www.Zibbet.com/Egilpatr

JULY

1 _____

2 _____

3 _____

4 _____

5 _____

6 _____

7 _____

8 _____

9 _____

10 _____

11 _____

12 _____

13 _____

14 _____

15 _____

16 _____

JULY

17 _____

18 _____

19 _____

20 _____

21 _____

22 _____

23 _____

24 _____

25 _____

26 _____

27 _____

28 _____

29 _____

30 _____

31 _____

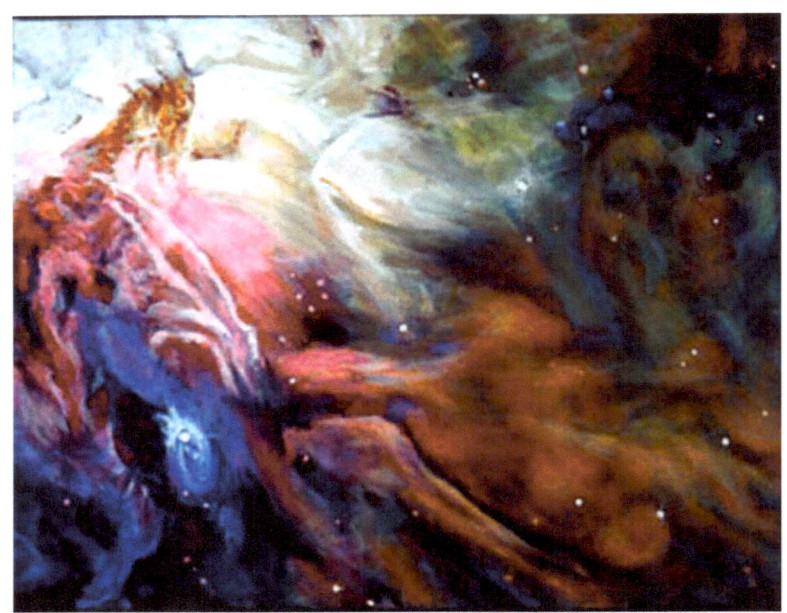

AUGUST

The Orion Nebula is based on a NASA photo of The Orion Nebula, named for the Galaxy of which the nebula is a part. This is an unimaginably huge part of the universe, where stars are being born. It invoked my love of space, free brush strokes, color, and form; and allowed me the joy of the abstract gesture within a framework of realism.

The painting is 16 inches high by 20 inches wide, acrylic on stretched canvas, on heavy duty stretchers, with painted sides. It can be seen online at http://www.Zibbet.com/Egilpatr

AUGUST

1 _____

2 _____

3 _____

4 _____

5 _____

6 _____

7 _____

8 _____

9 _____

10 _____

11 _____

12 _____

13 _____

14 _____

15 _____

16 _____

AUGUST

*17*_____

*18*_____

*19*_____

*20*_____

*21*_____

*22*_____

*23*_____

*24*_____

*25*_____

*26*_____

*27*_____

*28*_____

*29*_____

*30*_____

*31*_____

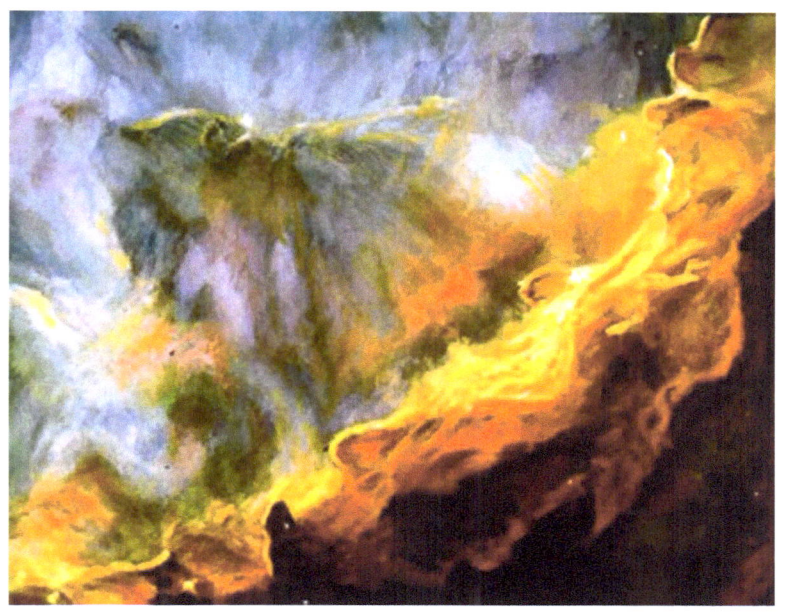

SEPTEMBER

The Swan Nebula is also based on a NASA photo. This is a part of the universe so large it cannot be imagined. There is an ocean of glowing hydrogen gas and small amounts of other elements such as oxygen and sulfur within the Swan Nebula. I was able to focus on and indulge my love of color, free brush strokes, and motion. I could concentrate on the joy of the abstract gesture within a framework of realism.

The painting is acrylic, 16 inches high by 20 inches wide, on stretched canvas, on heavy duty stretchers, with painted sides. The original painting is listed online at http://www.Zibbet.com/Egilpatr

SEPTEMBER

1_____

2_____

3_____

4_____

5_____

6_____

7_____

8_____

9_____

10_____

11_____

12_____

13_____

14_____

15_____

16_____

SEPTEMBER

17_____

18_____

19_____

20_____

21_____

22_____

23_____

24_____

25_____

26_____

27_____

28_____

29_____

30_____

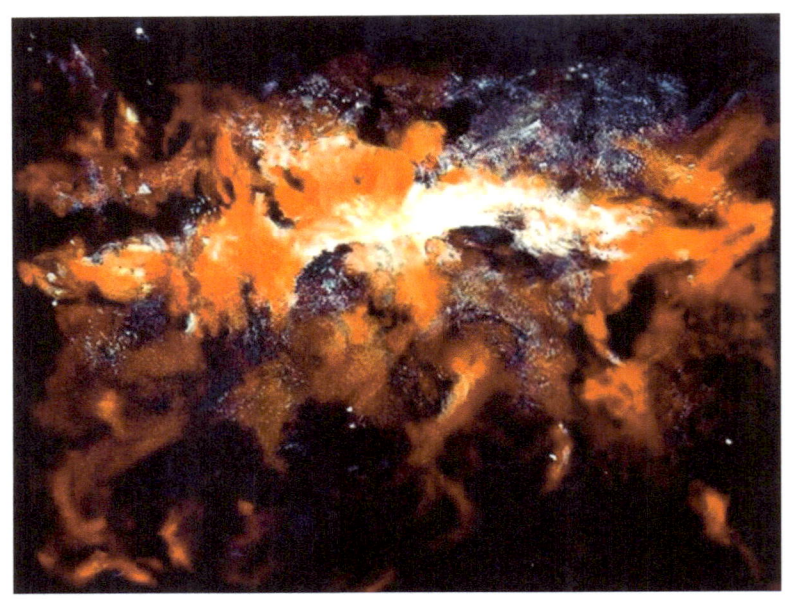

OCTOBER

The Milky Way is another painting based on a NASA space photo. Who could imagine a red "milky way"? As with the nebulas, the abstract nature of the forms and subject matter excited the realist painter in me, and offered a chance to let the brushwork take off.

The painting is 16 inches high by 20 inches wide, acrylic on stretched canvas, on heavy duty stretchers, with painted sides. See it at http://www.Zibbet.com/Egilpatr

OCTOBER

1_____

2_____

3_____

4_____

5_____

6_____

7_____

8_____

9_____

10_____

11_____

12_____

13_____

14_____

15_____

16_____

OCTOBER

17 _____

18 _____

19 _____

20 _____

21 _____

22 _____

23 _____

24 _____

25 _____

26 _____

27 _____

28 _____

29 _____

30 _____

31 _____

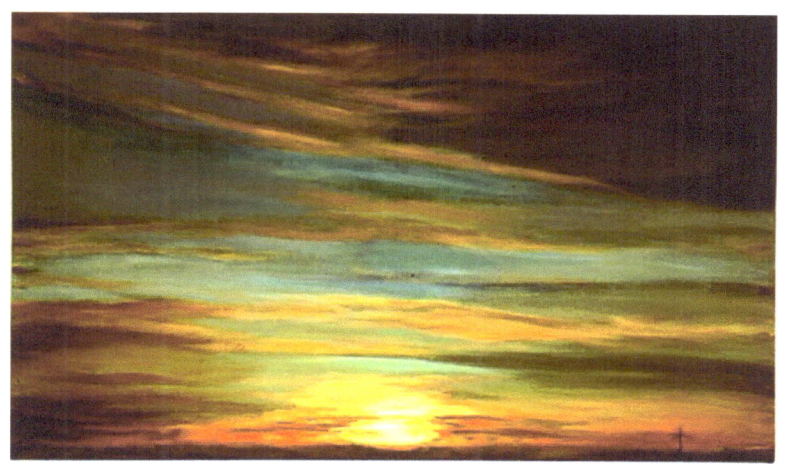

NOVEMBER

Albuquerque Sunset was created after my visit to a long lost, ex-sister in law, to whom I will forever be grateful for the chance to discover Albuquerque and Santa Fe, New Mexico. This was a sunset seen from a fourth floor apartment in Albuquerque. I was captured by the lights in the sky in this flat part of town, and a distant utility pole, and came up with my first abstract sunset.

The painting is 28 inches high by 46 inches wide, acrylic on stretched canvas, on heavy duty stretchers, with painted sides. See it at http://www.Zibbet.com/Egilpatr

NOVEMBER

1 _____

2 _____

3 _____

4 _____

5 _____

6 _____

7 _____

8 _____

9 _____

10 _____

11 _____

12 _____

13 _____

14 _____

15 _____

16 _____

NOVEMBER

17 _____

18 _____

19 _____

20 _____

21 _____

22 _____

23 _____

24 _____

25 _____

26 _____

27 _____

28 _____

29 _____

30 _____

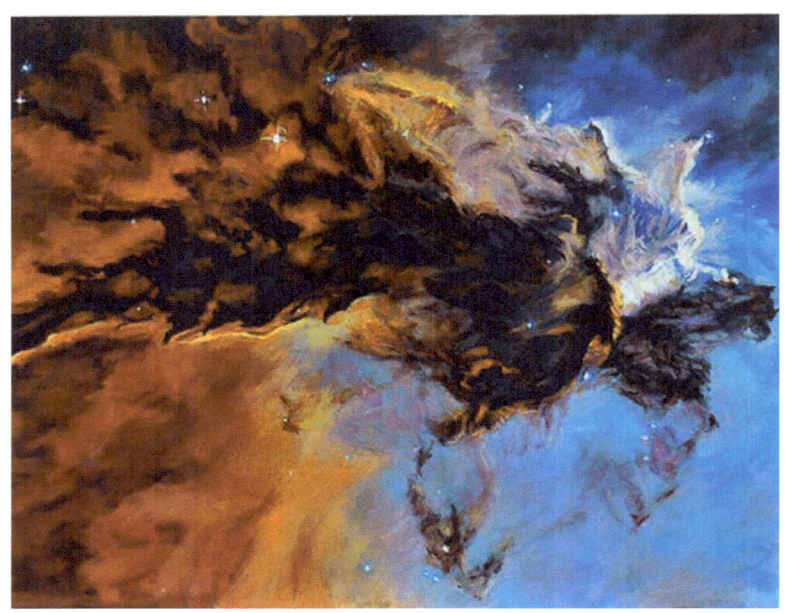

DECEMBER

The Eagle Nebula is based on a NASA photo that shows a vertical image. But I see the eagle when I place the image horizontally, and that is how I painted it, in love with the motion. As in all the nebula series I get the joy of free, abstract brushstrokes within a realist context.

The Eagle Nebula is in the constellation Serpens, a young, open cluster of a few thousand stars that were formed from a giant molecular cloud. They are still loosely bound to each other by gravitation, and active star formation is still going on.

The painting is 16 inches high by 20 inches wide, acrylic on stretched canvas, on heavy duty stretchers, with painted sides. It can be seen at a website online at: http://www.Zibbet.com/Egilpatr

DECEMBER

1 _____

2 _____

3 _____

4 _____

5 _____

6 _____

7 _____

8 _____

9 _____

10 _____

11 _____

12 _____

13 _____

14 _____

15 _____

16 _____

DECEMBER

17 _____

18 _____

19 _____

20 _____

21 _____

22 _____

23 _____

24 _____

25 _____

26 _____

27 _____

28 _____

29 _____

30 _____

31 _____

BIOGRAPHY

Eleanor Gilpatrick is a contemporary realist, painting landscapes, figural works, abstracts, and still lifes that capture fragments of the world. They arrest the viewer in terms of composition, color, and content. Illustrated in this book are some of her abstract and still life paintings, and Nebula paintings inspired by NASA photographs.

Prior to her art career, Eleanor Gilpatrick was professor at the School of Health Sciences, Hunter College, City University of New York.

She won prizes for painting and draftsmanship in high school and at the Educational Alliance in New York City, but chose to study the social sciences in college and graduate school. She eventually became an expert in health care policy and human resources, authored four books, directed a masters program in health services administration, and pioneered courses in critical thinking and writing. She is Professor Emerita at Hunter College.

Gilpatrick picked up the thread of drawing and painting in 1998 in plein-air workshops in Italy, and returned to serious study in studio courses at Hunter College just before she retired. An inventory of her paintings is on display at: http://www.Zibbet.com/Egilpatr

www.ingramcontent.com/pod-product-compliance
Lightning Source LLC
Chambersburg PA
CBHW041143180526
45159CB00002BB/717

* 9 7 8 1 4 4 8 6 7 5 7 0 8 *